A MURMUR OF BEES

In the name of the bee
And of the butterfly
And of the breeze
    Amen

       Emily Dickinson

A MURMUR
OF BEES

compiled by
AMORET SCOTT

with illustrations by
Dodie Masterman

THE OXFORD ILLUSTRATED PRESS

First published in 1980 by
Oxford Illustrated Press Ltd

© Amoret Scott and The Oxford Illustrated Press, 1980

Set in 10/12pt Plantin by Oxprint Ltd, Oxford
Printed and bound in Britain by
Butler and Tanner Ltd, Frome, Somerset
for Oxford Illustrated Press Ltd
Shelley Close, Headington
Oxford OX3 8HB

British Library Cataloguing in Publication Data
A murmur of bees.
    1. Bees—Literary collections
    2. English literature
I. Scott, Amoret
820′.8′036   PR1111.B/

ISBN 0-902280-79-1

CONTENTS

Acknowledgements	6
The Honey Bee	7
Honey (1)	10
The Educational Bee	16
The Amorous Bee	20
Weather Forecasting	32
Telling the Bees	38
The Honeycomb	50
Swarming	55
Athol Brose	60
The Profitable Bee	66
Honey (2)	76
Beeswax	80
Bears and Bees	84
Index of authors and first lines	93

ACKNOWLEDGEMENTS

For permission to reprint copyright material in this anthology my thanks are due to:
The National Trust and Macmillan London Ltd. 'The Bee-Boy's Song' by Rudyard Kipling. Jonathan Cape Ltd the extract from Book IV of The Georgics of Virgil translated by C. Day Lewis. Methuen Children's Books Ltd the extract from Winnie-the-Pooh by A. A. Milne. A. M. Heath & Co Ltd, for 'Sing a Song of Honey' by Barbara Euphan Todd. The Literary Trustees of Walter de la Mare and the Society of Authors as their representatives for 'The Bees' Song' by Walter de la Mare. William Heinemann Ltd the extract from 'The Bee Master' in The Land by V. Sackville-West. Macmillan London Ltd the extract from The Bee Oracles, part 1, from the Collected Poems of Edith Sitwell. Olwyn Hughes for 'The Beekeeper's Daughter' from The Colossus by Sylvia Plath, published Faber & Faber, copyright Ted Hughes 1971; and 'The Arrival of the Bee Box' from Ariel by Sylvia Plath, copyright Ted Hughes 1965. Hodder & Stoughton Ltd the extract from The Naked Runner by Francis Clifford. The Bulletin, Sydney, Australia, for 'Bees' by Roland Robinson. The Trustees for the Copyrights of the late Dylan Thomas for 'The Triolet'. The Poetry Society of America for 'The Bee' by John Fandel. David Lawson for 'The Bees' by Lola Ridge. Oxford University Press for 'Wild Bees' by James K. Baxter.

I would also like to record my gratitude for their patience and help to Mrs I. E. Allen at the International Bee Research Association library, Jean Kemsley, Laura Carter, and Alison Freegard.

THE HONEY BEE

The mysterious ways of the honey bee have fascinated man for over nine thousand years and among puzzles still unsolved is why this small insect should provide a link with major civilisations and religions throughout the world. Legends in the East and the West maintain that the bee is the messenger of the gods; this may have originated in Wales where it is accepted that when Adam and Eve were thrown out of the Garden of Eden the bees accompanied them—but with an all-important blessing instead of a curse. The Muslims expect to find the bee in Paradise and they also believe that she is the only animal addressed personally by God.

Today the bee's role as celestial messenger continues in the well-known practice on both sides of the Atlantic of 'telling the bees' about the fortunes and misfortunes of their owners. As

John Greenleaf Whittier shows, the English settlers who introduced the honey bee to America in the seventeenth century also brought the necessary lore for her well-being.

In the East such deities as Krishna and Siva are associated with the bee and the Indian god of Love, Kama, like Eros, carries a bow but 'on that bow, the lustrous string is made of bees'. Mohammedans too find that the Prophet emphasises the importance of the bee and he has named one of the books of the Koran after her.

As the divine origin of bees is so widely accepted, it is a logical extension to believe that their honey be considered the food of the gods and, by eating this, man too can achieve immortality. For many thousands of years honey was the sole sweetener used in cooking and the

> 'Cheese-cakes, steeped most thoroughly
> In the rich honey of the golden bee'

mentioned by Euripedes were only one of many delicacies which are still popular in Eastern Mediterranean countries. Special honey cakes were an important feature in religious rites and festivals; they are also reported to have been the sops which were thrown to pacify Cerberus, the three-headed guardian dog of the underworld. Sumerian scribes listed honey as one of the vital ingredients in the drug prescriptions they scratched on the earliest recorded clay writing tablets. And further virtues include its value as a talisman against snake poison, for exorcising demons and for preserving the dead.

In Australia it is the native stingless bees which are the subject of legend and poetry. Some of these do produce honey and as Percy Mumbulla relates, both the honey and the bee-grubs are a highly prized food of the Aboriginals. Although the honey bee was introduced in 1820, it would be a foolhardy man who questioned whether the living beard sported by Bowes, the hero of the ballad, was composed of fully armed immigrants or harmless natives. Bowes was continuing the tradition of the

8

itinerant David Wildman who visited the courts of Europe in the eighteenth century similarly demonstrating his confidence in a swarm. Then as now, it is a performance which guarantees a rapid round of drinks and cash from the nervous spectators.

In spite of the long history of bee-keeping and the past importance of both honey and wax to the economy of many countries, little progress in the scientific study of the craft was made until the seventeenth century. It was the poets, naturalists and philosophers whose curiosity and admiration were aroused by such a highly organised and industrious creature. There are many delights to be found in reading their observations and theories and this anthology, prompted by the same admiration, gives an essentially personal selection of poetry, prose and doggerel which the bee has inspired over the past three thousand years. Many writers have repeated fallacies from centuries earlier and often the naturalists' ideas are as charming as they are inaccurate. Sometimes they reveal a glimpse of the attitudes and practices then current: the eighteenth-century poet James Thomson vividly described the horrors of the annual destruction of the swarms by suffocation over a sulphur pit.

Bee-keeping has become increasingly popular in the last few years and the time may soon return when travellers in England remark once again on the hives at every cottage door. The adage that 'honey and wax give the two noblest things—sweetness and light' no longer applies now that sugar and electricity are readily available, but the virtues of the bee as extolled by the eighteenth- and nineteenth-century moralists are still valid today. Two thousand years ago the ancient Egyptians taught the importance of honey in healing ointments; today leading London medical schools continue to advocate its use for wounds which will not respond to modern drugs. It seems that some of the mysteries remain too.

HONEY

Honey is engendered from the air, mostly at the rising of the constellations, and more especially when Sirius is shining; . . . Whether it is that this liquid is the sweat of the heavens, or whether a saliva emanating from the stars, or a juice exuding from the air while purifying itself—would that it had been, when it comes to us, pure, limpid, and genuine, as it was when first it took its downward descent. But, as it is, falling from so vast a height, attracting corruption in its passage, and tainted by the exhalations of the earth as it meets them; sucked, too, as it is, from off the trees and the herbage of the fields, and accumulated in the stomachs of the bees, for they cast it up again through the mouth; deteriorated besides by the juices of flowers, and then steeped within the hives and subjected to such repeated changes: still, in spite of all this, it affords us by its flavour a most

10

exquisite pleasure, the result, no doubt, of its aethereal nature and origin.

PLINY THE ELDER
AD 23–79

See how much brighter my eyes are now that I have eaten this mouthful of honey.

I SAMUEL

Lovely, aerial blessing, which the bees
Fashion of plastic wax and fix with ease;
Free gift to man, whence many blessings flow,
Without the aid of sickle, axe or hoe.
Only a little trough where they may pour
The liquid sweets profuse of every flower:
Blessings be yours; may flowers your wanderings meet,
Ye winged workers of ethereal sweet.

ANTIPHILUS OF BYZANTIUM, c. AD 15

My son, eat thou honey, for it is good.

SOLOMON
Proverbs 24:13

The Prophet said:

Honey is a remedy for every illness, and the Koran is a remedy for all illnesses of the mind, therefore I recommend to you both remedies, the Koran and honey.

IBN MAGIH
?13th century

Thy Lord has taught the bee saying, 'provide thee houses in the mountains, and in the trees, and in the hives which men do build for thee. Feed, moreover, on every kind of fruit, and walk the beaten paths of the Lord'. From its belly cometh forth a fluid of varying hues, which yieldeth medicine for men. Verily in this is a sign for those who consider.

The Book of the Bee in the Koran

12

A charm against snake poison:

With the charm that was found of yore by the Brahmans . . .
with honey do I mix the rivers; the mountain peaks are honey.
Honey are the rivers, Parushni and Sipala. Prosperity be to thy
mouth, prosperity to thy heart.

> *Artharva-Veda* vi. 12
> Sacred Books of the East, c. 1000 BC

If thou hast founden honey, ete of it that suffyseth; for if
thou ete of it out of mesure, thou shalt spewe.

> GEOFFREY CHAUCER
> ?1340–1400

Honnie taken excessivelye cloyeth the stomache.

> JOHN LYLY, 1580

Lick up the honey and ask no questions.

> ARABIC

Well then, let me speak of the natural gifts that God himself
Bestowed on the bees, their reward
For obeying the charms—the chorus and clashing brass of the
      priests
And feeding the king of heaven when he hid in that Cretan cave,
They alone have their children in common, a city united
Beneath one roof and a life under established laws:
They know a native country, are sure of hearth and home.
Aware that winter is coming, they use the summer days
For work, and put their winnings into a common pool.
Some are employed in getting food, and by fixed agreement
Work on the fields: some stay within their fenced abode,
With tear of daffodil and gummy resin of tree-bark
Laying the first foundation of the honeycomb, then hanging
The stickfast wax: others bring up the young bees, the hope
Of their people: others press

14

The pure honey and cram the cells with that crystal nectar.
Some, allotted the duty of sentry-go at the gates,
Keep an eye out for showers and a sign of clouds in heaven,
Relieve incoming bees of their burden, or closing ranks
Shoo the drones—that work-shy gang—away from the bee-
    folds.
The work goes on like wildfire, the honey smells of thyme.
Thus when the Blacksmith Giants work double shifts to forge
Thunderbolts out of the stubborn ore, some ply the bellows
Of bull-skin, and others plunge the hissing metal in troughs:
And while Mount Aetna moans beneath their anvils' stress
They raise their arms with the powerful alternate rhythm of
    cranks,
They keep the iron turning in the close grip of their tongs.
So, to compare small things
With great, an inborn love of possession impels the bees
Each to his own office. The old are the town's wardens,
Who wall the honeycombs and frame the intricate houses.
Tired, as the night deepens, the young return from labour,
Their legs laden with thyme: they feed afar on the arbute,
The silvery willow, the spurge laurel, the fire-blush saffron,
The lime blossom so rich, the rust-red martagon lily.
For one and all one work-time, and a like rest from work.
At morning they hurry from the hives, all helter-skelter: again,
When the Evening Star has told them to leave their meadow
    pasture,
They make for home, they refresh themselves. What a
    murmuring
You hear as they drone around their policies and doorsteps!
Later, they settle down in their cells for the night, a silence
Falls, a drowsy fatigue falls.

Book IV *The Georgics of Virgil*
translated by C. Day Lewis

THE EDUCATIONAL BEE

Divine Songs for Children XX:
Against Idleness and Mischief

How doth the little busy bee
Improve each shining hour,
And gather honey all the day
From every opening flower!

How skilfully she builds her cell;
How neat she spreads the wax!
And labours hard to store it well
With the sweet food she makes.

ISAAC WATTS
1674–1748

The busy bee has no time for sorrow.

WILLIAM BLAKE, *Proverbs of Hell*, 1808

16

What Do They Do?

What does the Bee do?
Bring home honey.
And what does Father do?
Bring more money.
And what does Mother do?
Lay out the money.
And what does baby do?
Eat up the honey.

CHRISTINA ROSSETTI
1830–1894

Riddle Rhyme

There is a bird of great renown,
Useful in city and in town;
None work like unto him can do;
He's yellow, black, red, and green,
A very pretty bird I mean;
Yet he's both fierce and fell:
I count him wise that can this tell.

Answer: A bee

16th century MS

Great God Almighty in thy pretty Bee,
Mine Eie (as written in small letters) sees
An Abstract of that Wisdome, Power and Love
Which is imprinted on the Heav'ns above
In larger Volumes, for their eies to see,
That in such little prints behold not Thee,
And in this workmanship (oh Lord) of thine,
I praise thy Wisdome and thy Power divine.

GEORGE WITHER
1588–1667

So work the honey bees,
Creatures that by a rule in nature teach
The act of order to a peopled kingdom.
They have a king and officers of sorts;
Where some, like magistrates, correct at home;
Others, like merchants, venture trade abroad;
Others, like soldiers, armed in their stings,
Make boot upon the summer's velvet buds,
Which pillage they with merry march bring home
To the tent royal of their emperor
Who, busied in his majesty, surveys
The singing masons building roofs of gold,
The civil citizens kneading up the honey,
The poor mechanic porters crowding in
Their heavy burdens at his narrow gate,
The sad-ey'd justice, with his surly hum,
Delivering o'er to executors pale
The lazy yawning drone.

Henry V, I ii
WILLIAM SHAKESPEARE
1564–1616

18

All hands employ'd, the royal work grows warm
Like lab'ring bees on a long summer's day,
Some sound the trumpet for the rest to swarm
And some on bells of tasted lilies play;
With glewy wax some new foundations lay
Of virgin comb, which from the roof are hung,
Or tend the sick, or educate the young.

JOHN DRYDEN
1631–1700

Upon the Bee

The bee goes out, and honey home doth bring;
And some who seek that honey find a sting.
Now would'st thou have the honey, and be free
From stinging; in the first place kill the bee.

Comparison
This bee an emblem truly is of sin,
Whose sweet unto a many, death hath been,
Would'st thou have sweet from sin, and not die,
Sin in the first place thou must mortify.

JOHN BUNYAN
1628–1688

THE AMOROUS BEE

The captiv'd Bee: or, The little Filcher

As Julia once a-slumb'ring lay,
It chanc't a Bee did flie that way,
(After a dew, or dew-like shower)
To tipple freely in a flower.
For some rich flower, he took the lip
Of Julia, and began to sip;

But when he felt he suckt from thence
Hony, and in the quintessence:
He drank so much he scarce co'd stir;
So Julia took the Pilferer.
And thus surpriz'd (as Filchers use)
He thus began himselfe t'excuse:
Sweet Lady-Flower, I never brought
Hither the least one theeving thought:
But taking those rare lips of yours
For some fresh, fragrant, luscious flowers:
I thought I might there take a taste,
Where so much sirrop ran at waste.
Besides, know this, I never sting

The flower that gives me nourishing:
But with a kisse, or thanks, doe pay
For Honie, that I beare away.
This said, he laid his little scrip
Of hony, 'fore her Ladiship:
And told her, (as some tears did fall)
That, that he took, and that was all.
At which she smil'd; and bade him goe
And take his bag; but thus much know,
When next he came a pilfring so,
He sho'd from her full lips derive,
Hony enough to fill his hive.

ROBERT HERRICK
1591–1674

When a couple are newly married, the first moneth is honey-moon or smick smack; the second is, hither and thither; the third is, thwick thwack; the fourth, the Devil take them that brought thee and I together.

JOHN RAY, 1670

Where honey, there is gall.

Favourite saying of MARTIN LUTHER

21

The Bee—*A Song*

A busy humble Bee am I,
That range the garden sunny,
From flower to flower I changing fly,
And every flower's my honey.
Bright Chloe with her golden hair,
A while my rich Jonquil is,
'Till cloy'd with sipping Nector there,
I shift to rosy Phillis.
I shift to rosy Phillis

But Phillis's sweet opening breast,
Remains not long my station;
For Kitty now must be addrest,
My pretty spic'd Carnation:
Yet Kitty's fragrant bed I'd leave,
To other flowers I'm rover;
And all in turns my love receive,
The gay wide garden over.
The gay wide garden over.

Variety that knows no bounds,
My roving fancy edges,
And oft with Flora I am found,
In dalliance under hedges.
For as I am an errant BEE

22

Who range each bank that's sunny,
Both fields and gardens are my fee,
And every flower my honey.
And every flower my honey.

ANON, c. 1700

Hony-moon, applyed to those marryed persons that love well at first, and decline in affection afterwards; it is hony now, but it will change as the Moon.

THOMAS BLOUNT, 1656

When the nest is destroyed others get the honey.

CHINESE

Ah, see where, robb'd and murder'd in that pit,
Lies the still-heaving hive, at evening snatch'd
Beneath the cloud of guilt concealing night,
And fix'd o'er sulphur; while not dreaming ill,
The happy people in their waxen cells
Sat tending public cares, and planning schemes
Of temperance, for winter poor, rejoiced
To mark, full flowing round, their copious store.
Sudden the dark oppressive steam ascends,
And, used to milder scent, the tender race
By thousands tumble from their honeyed domes,
Convolv'd and agonising in the dust.
And was it then for this you roam'd the Spring
Intent from flower to flower; for this you toil'd
Ceaseless the burning Summer heats away;
For this in Autumn search'd the blooming waste,
Nor lost one sunny gleam? For this sad fate?
Ah, man, tyrranic lord, how long, how long
Shall prostrate nature groan beneath your rage,
Awaiting renovation, when obliged
Must you destroy? Of their ambrosial food
Can you not borrow, and in just return
Afford them shelter from the wintry winds;
Or, as the sharp year pinches, with their own
Again regale them on some smiling day?

24

See where the stony bottom of their town,
Looks desolate and wild; with here and there
A helpless member, who the ruin'd state
Survives, lamenting, weak, cast out to death.

JAMES THOMSON
1700–1748

Ode to the Bee

Herds, blythsome tune your canty[†] reeds,   *cheerful*
And welcome to the gowany[†] meads   *daisied*
The pride o' a' the insect thrang,
A stranger to the green sae lang.
Unfald ilk buss[†] and ilka brier,   *bush*
The bounties o' the gleesom year,
To him whase voice delights the spring,
Whase soughs[†] the saftest slumbers bring.   *moans*
   Whan fields ha'e got their dewy gift,
And dawnin breaks upo' the lift,
Then gang ye're wa's thro' hight and how,

Seek caller haugh[†] or sunny know[†],   *valleys*   *hillock*
Or ivy'd craig, or burnbank brae,
Whare industry shall bid ye gae,
For hiney or for waxen store,
To ding sad poortith[†] frae your door,   *poverty*
   Cou'd feckless creature, man, be wise,
The simmer o' his life to prize,
In winter he might fend fu' bald,
His eild unkend to nippin' cald,
Yet thir, alas! are antrin fock
That lade their scape wi' winter stock.
Auld age maist feckly glowrs right dour
Upo' the ailings of the poor,
Wha hope for nae comforting, save
That dowie[†] dismal house, the grave.   *gloomy*
Then feeble man, be wise, take tent[†]   *head*
How industry can fetch content:
Behad the bees whare'er they wing,
Or thro' the bonny bow'rs of spring,
Whare vi'lets or whare roses blaw,
And siller[†] dew-draps nightly fa',   *silver*
Or whan on open bent they're seen,
On hether-bell or thristle green;
The hiney's still as sweet that flows
Frae thistle cald or kendling rose.
   Frae this the human race may learn
Reflection's hiney'd draps to earn,
Whither they tramp life's thorny way,
Or thro' the sunny vineyard stray.
   Instructive bee! attend me still,
O'er a' my labours sey your skill:
For thee shall hiney-suckles rise,
With lading to your busy thighs,
And ilka shrub surround my cell,

26

Whereon ye like to hum and dwell:
My trees in bourachs† o'er my ground   *groups*
Shall fend ye frae ilk blast o' wind;
Nor e'er shall herd, wi' ruthless spike,
Delve out the treasures frae your bike,†   *hives*
But in my fence be safe, and free
To live, and work, and sing like me.

ROBERT FERGUSSON
1750–1774

To a Honey Bee

Thou, born to sip the lake or spring,
  Or quaff the waters of the stream,
Why hither come, on vagrant wing?
    Does Bacchus tempting seem—
      Did he for you this glass prepare?
      Will I admit you to a share?

Did storms harass or foes perplex,
  Did wasps or king-birds bring dismay—
Did wars distress, or labors vex,

27

Or did you miss your way?
   A better seat you could not take
   Than on the margin of this lake.

Welcome! I hail you to my glass:
   All welcome here you find;
Here let the cloud of trouble pass,
   Here be all care resigned.
     This fluid never fails to please,
     And drown the griefs of men or bees.

What forced you here we cannot know,
   And you will scarcely tell,
But cheery we would have you go
   And bid a glas farewell:
     On lighter wings we bid you fly—
     Your dart will now all foes defy.

Yet take not, oh! too deep a drink,
   And in this ocean die;
Here bigger bees than you might sink,
   Even bees full six feet high.
     Like Pharoah, then, you would be said
     To perish in a sea of red.

Do as you please, your will is mine;
   Enjoy it without fear,
And your grave will be this glass of wine,
   Your epitaph—a tear;
     Go, take your seat in Charon's boat;
     We'll tell the hive, you died afloat.

PHILIP FRENEAU
1752–1832

28

Where the cherry spreads its flowery tufts,
'Tis pleasure to survey the snowy pomp,
And pause in contemplating of the hum
Of mingled bees industrious, that invade
And rifle in succession every flower;
Some large and gifted with the voice profound
Of mellow bass, some with the loftier pipe
Of tenor soft, of small soprano some,
That fancy oft may deem she hears distinct,
The sweet coincidence of fellow-tones
Producing harmony's full chord divine.

JAMES HURDIS
1763–1801

Thou art a miser, thou busy busy bee,
Late and early at employ;
Still on thy golden stores intent,
Thy summer in reaping and hoarding is spent
What thy winter will never enjoy:
What lesson this for me, thou busy busy bee!

Little dost thou think, thou busy busy bee,
What is the end of thy toil,
When the latest flowers of the ivy are gone,
And all thy work for the year is done,
Thy master comes for the spoil:
Woe then for thee, thou busy busy bee!

ROBERT SOUTHEY
1774–1843

Invitation to the Bee

Child of patient industry,
Little active busy bee,
Thou are out at early morn,
Just as the opening flowers are born,
Among the green and grassy meads
Where the cowslips hang their heads;
Or by hedgerows, while the dew
Glitters on the harebell blue.

Then on eager wing art flown
To thymy hillocks on the down;
Or to revel on the broom;
Or suck the clover's crimson bloom;
Murmuring still, thou busy bee,
Thy little ode to industry.

Go while summer suns are bright,
Take at large thy wandering flight;
Go and load thy tiny feet
With every rich and various sweet;
Cling around the flowering thorn,
Dive in the woodbine's honeyed horn,
Seek the wild rose that shades the dell,
Explore the foxglove's freckled bell,
Or in the heath flower's fairy cup
Drink the fragrant spirit up.

But when the meadows shall be mown,
And summer's garlands overblown;
Then come, thou little busy bee,
And let thy homestead be with me;
There, sheltered by thy straw-built hive,
In my garden thou shalt live,
And that garden shall supply
Thy delicious alchemy.

CHARLOTTE SMITH
1749–1806

31

WEATHER FORECASTING

Insects also are very sensible of such changes of weather:. . .
But the surest and most certain sign is taken from bees, which
are more incommoded by rain than almost any other creatures,
and therefore, as soon as the air begins to grow heavy, and the
vapours to condense, they will not fly from their hives, but
either remain in them all day, or else fly but to a small distance.

The Shepherd of Banbury's rules to judge of the
changes of the weather grounded on Forty Years
Experience
JOHN CLARIDGE, 1765

Bees will not swarm
Before a near storm.

When bees to distance wing their flight,
Days are warm and skies are bright;
But when their flight ends near their home,
Stormy weather is sure to come.

If rain threatens, be sure they'll not roam too far afield
From their hives: they mistrust the sky, should an east wind be
        due:
At such times safely beneath the walls of their town they forage
Around, making brief excursions, and often carry some ballast,
As dinghies do to stiffen them in a high sea—they lift
Wee stones, and with these they weather the cloud-tossed
        solitudes.

VIRGIL
70–19 BC

A bee was never caught in a shower.

If bees stay at home,
Rain will soon come;
If they fly away,
Fine will be the day.

Formidable Attack by Bees

A true account as narrated in the *Berliner Zeitung* in 1820.

On the 20th of July, M. Eulert, a merchant of Berlin, was travelling with his wife from Wittenberg to that city; they were in a private carriage, and a coachman was driving. While passing along the high-road, between Kroppstadt and Schmogelsdorf, the coachman observed the horses to rub uneasily against each other, as if stung by a horse-fly. Suddenly a swarm of bees appeared, or a collection of swarms, numerous beyond all reckoning. They covered the carriages, horses, travellers, and coachman, but especially the living beings. They attacked the mouth, nose, eyes and ears of each horse, until the poor animals, quite overcome, lay down unresisting. The coachman lost his hat while endeavouring to aid the horses, and the bees then fastened upon his head with such avidity, that his poor skull became covered with a matted mass of bees, hair and blood; he threw himself on the ground in desperation, and became for a time insensible.

Madame Eulert, as soon as the attack began, covered her face with her hood, got out of the carriage, hastened to a neighbouring field, and threw herself, face downwards, on the grass. M. Eulert then alighted, and shouted for help; but while his mouth was open, some of the bees entered it, and increased his troubles. He then covered his face and neck with a handkerchief, and ran to a place where he saw three peasants, looking on; but they were too much alarmed to help him, and so he ran on further. He then met a woodman, a carrier with a cart, and three horses, and some labourers. After much entreaty, the carrier agreed to put his horses into a neighbouring stable, and to accompany M. Eulert, as did the others, all carrying dry hay and straw to burn. Arrived at the spot, they found Madame

Eulert still lying, face downward, on the grass, very little injured. The poor coachman was lying nearly insensible, and for forty-eight hours his case was precarious.

After burning much hay and straw to drive away the bees, M. Eulert and his helpers were able to examine the suffering horses; one was so maddened by the stinging it had received, that it died the same day; the other was taken to Schmogelsdorf and placed under the care of a veterinary surgeon, but the poor animal died on the following day. M. Eulert, in attempting afterwards to assign a probable reason for this fierce attack, supposed that when the horses had been seen to be against each other, a queen-bee was annoying one of them; that the rubbing crushed her; and that the attack by the swarm was an expression of the bees' resentment for the murder of their queen.

. . . .

Naturalists who have studied the extraordinary habits and instincts of bees have not yet succeeded in discovering the various circumstances which lead those insects to attack man in a hostile spirit. How far revenge, or retaliation for injuries received, influences them is but imperfectly known.

Swine, women and bees are not to be turned.

Honey is sweet but the bee stings.

GERMAN

There was an Old Man in a tree,
Who was horribly bored by a bee;
When they said, 'Does it buzz?'
He replied, 'Yes, it does!
It's a regular brute of a bee!

EDWARD LEAR
1812–1888

God's little epigrams, the Bees
Are pointed and impartial.
Could Martial rival one of them?
No, not even Martial.

RICHARD KIRK

TELLING THE BEES

Telling the Bees

Here is the place; right over the hill
   Runs the path I took;
You can see the gap in the old wall still,
   And the stepping-stones in the shallow brook.

There is the house, with the gate red-barred,
   And the poplars tall;
And the barn's brown length, and the cattle-yard,
   And the white horns tossing above the wall.

There are the beehives ranged in the sun;
   And down by the brink

Of the brook are her poor flowers, weed-o'errun,
  Pansy and daffodil, rose and pink.

A year has gone, as the tortoise goes,
  Heavy and slow;
And the same rose blows, and the same sun glows,
  And the same brook sings of a year ago.

There's the same sweet clover-smell in the breeze;
  And the June sun warm
Tangles his wings of fire in the trees,
  Setting, as then, over Fernside farm.

I mind me how with a lover's care
  From my Sunday coat
I brushed off the burrs, and smoothed my hair,
  And cooled at the brookside my brow and throat.

Since we parted, a month had passed,—
  To love, a year;
Down through the beeches I looked at last
  On the little red gate and the well-seep near.

I can see it all now,—the slantwise rain
  Of light through the leaves,
The sundown's blaze on her window-pane,
  The bloom of her roses under the eaves.

Just the same as a month before,—
  The house and the trees,
The barn's brown gable, the vine by the door,—
  Nothing changed but the hives of bees.

Before them, under the garden wall,
  Forward and back,
Went drearily singing the chore-girl small,
  Draping each hive with a shred of black.

Trembling, I listened: the summer sun
    Had the chill of snow;
For I knew she was telling the bees of one
    Gone on the journey we all must go!

Then I said to myself, 'My Mary weeps
    For the dead to-day:
Haply her blind old grandsire sleeps
    The fret and the pain of his age away.'

But her dog whined low; on the doorway sill,
    With his cane to his chin,
The old man sat; and the chore-girl still
    Sang to the bees stealing out and in.

And the song she was singing ever since
    In my ear sounds on:—
'Stay at home, pretty bees, fly not hence!
    Mistress Mary is dead and gone!'

JOHN GREENLEAF WHITTIER
1807–1892

The Bee-Boy's Song

Bees! Bees! Hark to your bees!
'Hide from your neighbours as much as you please,
But all that has happened, to *us* you must tell,
Or else we will give you no honey to sell!'

      A maiden in her glory,
        Upon her wedding-day,
      Must tell her Bees the story,
        Or else they'll fly away.
        Fly away—die away—

Dwindle down and leave you!
But if you don't deceive your Bees,
    Your Bees will not deceive you.

Marriage, birth or buryin',
    News across the seas,
All you're sad or merry in,
    You must tell the Bees.
        Tell'em coming in an' out,
            Where the Fanners fan,
        'Cause the Bees are just about
            As curious as a man!

Don't you wait where trees are,
    When the lightnings play,
Nor don't you hate where Bees are,
    Or else they'll pine away.

41

Pine away—dwine away—
    Anything to leave you!
But if you never grieve your Bees,
    Your Bees'll never grieve you.

RUDYARD KIPLING
1865–1936

Honey bees, honey bees, hear what I say!
Your Master J. A. has passed away.
But his wife now begs you will freely stay,
And still gather honey for many a day.
Bonny bees, bonny bees, hear what I say!

TRADITIONAL, LINCOLNSHIRE

Whist! Laatle bees, sad tidings I bear,
Bees, bees, murmurin' low;
Cauld i' his grave ligs your maister dear,
Bees, bees, murmurin' low;
Nae mair he'll ride t' soond o' t' honr,
Nae mair he'll fettle his sickle for t' corn,
Nea mair he'll coom to your skep of a morn,
Bees, bees, murmurin' low.

Look, conny[†] bees, I's winndin' black crape,   *darling*
Bees, bees, murmurin' low;
Slowly an' sadly your skep I mun drape,
Bees, bees, murmurin' low;
Else you will sicken an dwine[†] reet away,   *waste*
Heart-broken bees, now your maister is clay:
Or, mebbe, you'll leave us wi' t' dawn o' t' day,
Bees, bees, murmurin' low;

Sitha! I bring you your share o' the feast.
Bees, bees, murmurin' low;
Cakes an' yal[†] an' wine you mun taste,   *ale*
Bees, bees, murmurin' low;
Gie some to t' queen on her gowlden throne,
Ther's foison[†] to feed both worker an' drone;   *plenty*
Oh! dean't let us fend for oursels alone;
Bees, bees, murmurin' low.

F. W. MOORMAN
from 'Songs of the Ridings'

It does not appear from experiment that bees are in any way capable of being affected by sounds: for I have often tried my own with a large speaking-trumpet held close to their hives, and with such an exertion of voice as would have hailed a ship at a distance of a mile, and still these insects pursued their various employments, undisturbed and without showing the least sensibility or resentment.

(Letter xxxviii to Daines Barrington, *The Natural History of Selbourne*)
GILBERT WHITE
1720–1793

The bee is small among fowles, yet doth its fruite passe in sweetness.

ECCLESIASTES

The bee observe,
She too an artist is, and laughs at man,
Who calls on rules the sightly hexagon
With truth to form, a cunning architect,
Who at the roof begins her golden work,
And builds without foundation. How she toils.

JAMES HURDIS
1763–1801

Madam, the ancient proverb says . . .
That one rich drop of honey sweet,
As an alluring luscious treat,
Is known to tempt more flies by far
Than a whole tun of vinegar.

WILLIAM COMBE, *Dr Syntax in Search of a Wife*, 1821

I eat my peas with honey,
I've done it all my life.
It makes the peas taste funny,
But it keeps them on my knife.

ANON

Cupid once upon a bed
Of roses laid his weary head;
Luckless urchin, not to see
Within the leaves a slumbering bee!
The bee awaked—with anger wild
The bee awaked, and stung the child.
Loud and piteous are his cries;
To Venus quick he runs, he flies!
'O mother! I am wounded through,
I die with pain—in sooth I do!
Stung by some little, angry thing,
Some serpent on a tiny wing—
A bee it was,—for once, I know,
I heard a rustic call it so.'
Thus he spoke, and she the while
Heard him with a soothing smile;
Then said, 'My infant, if so much
Thou feel the little wild bee's touch,
How must the heart, oh Cupid! be
The Hapless heart that's stung by thee!'

THOMAS MOORE
1779–1852

46

The Brownie[†] Bee
A Cornish Croon

*fairy guardian
of bees*

Behold those winged images!
Bound for their evening bowers;
They are the nation of the bees,
Born from the breath of flowers!
Strange people they! A mystic race,
In life and food and dwelling place!

And once—it is a grandame's tale,
Yet filled with secret lore—
There dwelt within a woodland vale,
Fast by old Cornwall's shore,
An ancient woman, worn and bent,
Fallen Nature's mournful monument.

A home had they—the clustering race,
Beside her garden-wall;
All blossoms breathed around the place,
And sunbeams fain would fall;
The lily loved that combe the best,
Of all the valleys of the west!

But so it was that on a day,
When summer built her bowers,
The waxen wanderers ceased to play
Around the cottage flowers:
No hum was heard; no wing would roam;
They dwelt within their cloistered home!

This lasted long—no tongue could tell
Their pastime or their toil!
What binds the soldier to his cell,
Who should divide the spoil?
It lasted long—it fain would last,
Till Autumn rustled on the blast!

47

Then sternly went that woman old,
She sought the chancel floor:
And there, with purpose bad and bold,
Knelt down amid the poor:
She took, she hid, the blessed bread,
Which is, what Jesu master said!

She bare it to her distant home,
She laid it by the hive,—
To lure the wanderers forth to roam,
That so her store might thrive:
'Twas a wild wish, a thought unblest,
Some cruel legend of the west!

But lo! at morning-tide, a sign!
For wondering eyes to trace;
They found, above that bread, a shrine
Reared by the harmless race:
They brought their walls from bud and flower,
They built bright roof and beamy tower!

Was it a dream? or did they hear
Float from those golden cells,
A sound, as of some psaltery near,
Or soft and silvery bells?
A low, sweet psalm, that grieved within,
In mournful memory of the sin!

Was it a dream? 'tis sweet no less,
Set not the vision free;—
Long let the lingering legend bless,
The nation of the bee!
So shall they bear upon their wings,
A parable of sacred things!

So shall they teach, when men blaspheme,
Or sacrament or shrine,
That humbler things may fondly dream
Of mysteries divine:
And holier hearts than his may beat,
Beneath the bold blasphemer's feet!

R. S. H., c. 1860

And from the knotted flowers of thyme
When the woodland banks are deck't,
See the bee his load collect;
Mark him turn the petals by,
Gold-dust gathering on his thigh,
As full many a hum he heaves,
While he pats th' intruding leaves
Lost in many a heedless spring,
Then wearing home on weary wing.

JOHN CLARE
1793–1864

THE HONEYCOMB

Honey, as it is collected by the bees, is a perspiration of the sap of plants in particles which exude through the pores and condense on the flowers, or leaves. It has been inferred, from careful observations, that the bees make no alteration in the honey, but discharge it into their magazines or cells just as nature produced it on the flowers. That honey partakes of the flowers from which it is derived there can be no doubt, or that the newest is the best; but as to its taste and quality there is a variety of opinions.

JOHN MILTON, *The Practical Bee-Keeper*, 1843

Bees make honey and men eat it.

CHINESE

The Hony-combe

If thou hast found an honie-combe,
Eat thou not all, but taste on some:
For if thou eat'st it to excess;
That sweetness turnes to Loathsomness.
Taste it to Temper; then 'twill be
Marrow, and Manna unto thee.

ROBERT HERRICK
1591–1674

If you want to gather honey, don't kick over the beehive.

ABRAHAM LINCOLN
1809–1865

Wit is honey lent, without the sting.

ALFRED TENNYSON
1809–1892

White virgin honey comes from earliest flowers,
White virgin honey in the market prized;
From the white clover creeping in the field,
From orchard-blossom that the worker scours,
—The richest honey-flow of all the Weald,—
But cottage-gardens shall not be despised
Here where no heather is, and scanty lime;
Therefore, at evening, when the field-work's done,
And daylight lingers with the latening sun,
Let gardeners too remember sowing-time.

V. SACKVILLE-WEST
1892–1962

The hive is up in arms, expert to teach,
Nor proudly to be taught unwilling; each
Seems from her fellow a new zeal to catch;
Strength in her limbs, and on her wings despatch,
The bee goes forth; from herb to herb she flies,
From flow'r to flow'r, and loads the lab'ring thighs,
With treasured sweets, robbing those flow'rs which, left,
Find not themselves made poorer by the theft.
Ne'er doth she flit on pleasure's silken wing,
Ne'er doth she loit'ring let the bloom of spring
Unrifled pass, and on the downy breast
Of some fair flower indulge untimely rest.
Ne'er doth she, drinking deep of those rich dews
Which chymist night prepared, that faith abuse
Due to the hive, and selfish in her toils,
To her own private use convert the spoils.
Love of the stock first called her forth to roam,
And to the stock she brings her booty home.

CHARLES CHURCHILL
1731–1764

Julius Caesar and the Honey-Bee

Poring on Caesar's death with earnest eye,
I heard a fretful buzzing on the pane:
'Poor bee!' I cried, 'I'll help thee by and by';
Then dropped mine eyes upon the page again.
Alas, I did not rise; I helped him not;
In the great voice of Roman history
I lost the pleading of the window-bee,
And all his woes and troubles were forgot.
In pity for the mighty chief, who bled
Beside his rival's statue, I delayed
To serve the little insect's present need;
And so he died for lack of human aid.
I could not change the Roman's destiny;
I might have set the honey-maker free.

CHARLES TENNYSON TURNER
1808–1879

Thou cheerful bee! come, freely come,
And travel round my woodbine bower!
Delight me with thy wandering hum,
And rouse me from my musing hour!
Oh! try no more those tedious fields,
Come, taste the sweets my garden yields;
The treasures of each blooming mine,
The bud, the blossom, all are thine.

PROFESSOR SMYTHE

The Flesh-fly and the Bee

A bee upon a briar-rose hung
And wild with pleasure suck'd and kiss'd;
A flesh-fly near, with snout in dung,
Sneer'd, 'What a Transcendentalist!'

COVENTRY PATMORE
1823–1896

A Merry Bee

A golden bee a-cometh
O'er the mere, glassy mere,
And a merry tale he hummeth
In my ear.

How he seized and kiss'd a blossom
From its true thorny tree,
Pluck'd and placed in Annie's bosom,
Hums the bee!

JOSEPH SKIPSEY
1832–1903

SWARMING

Swarming Song

Bees, of Bees of Paradise,
Does the work of Jesus Christ,
Does the work that no man can,
God made man and man made money,
God made bees and bees make honey,
God made great men to plough and sow
And God made little boys to tend the rook and crow.

Hurra!

WEST SUSSEX, c. 1885

So on a Sabbath morn
Cloudy and calm, with not one sunny gleam
To lure them forth, I've seen a num'rous swarm
(Whether attracted by the silence deep
And pause of rural toil, or sudden struck
By that instinctive impulse which directs
More wisely than proud Reason's rule) rush out
In myriads and take wing: while mingling sounds
Of distant church-bells and the jangling pan
Essayed in vain to stop the living cloud.

(?) GRAHAME

A play o' bees in May's worth a noble the same day,
A play o' bees in June's purty soon,
A play o' bees in July's nod worth a butterfly.

TRADITIONAL, SHROPSHIRE

56

It being a proverb, that a swarm of bees in May is worth a cow and a bottle of hay, whereas a swarm in July is not worth a fly.

Reformed Commonwealth of Bees, 1655

A May's swarm is worth a mare's foal.

WILLIAM LAWSON, 1676

A swarm of bees in May,
Is worth a cow and calf that day;
A swarm of bees in June,
Is worth a silver spoon;
A swarm of bees in July
Is not a worth a butterfly.

TRADITIONAL, WEXFORD, IRELAND

Bee Proffers HONEY

A Knight of a gay and a gallant mien,
On a milk white courser came,
In his hat was a lady's favour seen,
For innocence knows no shame.
And he tapp'd at the fair lady's bower with glee,
She heard but impatience to mar,
When he cried 'fair lady come ride with me'
She answer'd him with her guitar,
Tink a tink, tink a tink tink a tink ting
The bee proffers honey but bears a sting.

A Knight with a dark and a scowling brow
On a cole black steed came by
He heard the two lovers exchange a vow,
And fury gave fire to his eyes,
But he courteously said if yo're crossed in love,
And would bear the fair lady afar
My sword and my service are yours to prove
But the lady she play'd her guitar,
Tink a tink, tink a tink tink a tink ting
The bee proffers honey but bears a sting.

The knight so gallant disappear'd that day
And never was heard of more,
And the sable knight made a proud display
Of the favour that gallant knight wore
The lady he woo'd but he gain'd no grace
And joy from his bosom went far,
For the honey of hope to guilt's sting gave place
And conscience still play'd the guitar,
Tink a tink, tink a tink tink a tink ting
The bee proffers honey but bears a sting.

ANON broadside in author's collection, c. 1820

A Bee his burnished Carriage

A Bee his burnished Carriage
Drove boldly to a Rose—
Combinedly alighting—
Himself— his Carriage was—
The Rose received his visit
With frank tranquility
Witholding not a Crescent
To his Cupidity—
Their Moment consummated—
Remained for him— to flee—
Remained for her— of rapture
But the humility.

EMILY DICKINSON
1830–1886

The pedigree of Honey
Does not concern the Bee,
Nor lineage of Ecstasy
Delay the Butterfly
On spangled journeys to the peak
Of some perceiveless thing—
The Right of way to Tripoli
A more essential thing.

EMILY DICKINSON
1830–1886

ATHOL BROSE

Charm'd with a drink which Highlanders compose,
A German traveller exclaim'd with glee,—
Potztausend! sare, if dis is Athol Brose,
How goot dere Athol Boetry must be!

THOMAS HOOD
1799–1845

Mantling in the goblet, see
The pure bev'rage of the bee.
O'er it hangs the shield of gold,
'Tis the drink of Balder bold.

THOMAS GRAY
1716–1771

Athole Brose

Willie an' I cam down by Blair
   And in by Tullibardine,
The kye were at the waterside,
   An' bee-skeps in the garden.
I saw the reek of a private still—
   Says I, 'Gud Lord, I thank ye!'
As Willie and I cam in by Blair
   And out by Killiecrankie.

Ye hinny bees, ye smuggler lads,
   Thou, Muse, the band's protector,
I never kent what kye were for
   Till I had drunk the nectar!
And shall I never drink it mair?
   Gud troth, I beg your pardon!
The neist time I come down by Blair
   And in by Tullibardine.

ROBERT LOUIS STEVENSON
1850–1894

61

The Bees' Song

Thousandz of thornz there be
On the Rozez where gozez
The Zebra of Zee:
Sleek, striped, and hairy,
The steed of the Fairy
Princess of Zee

Heavy with blossomz be
The Rozez that growzez
In the thickets of Zee,
Where grazez the Zebra
Marked *Abracadeeebra*
Of the Princess of Zee.

And he nozez the poziez
Of the Rozez that growzez
So luvez'm and free,
With an eye, dark and wary,
In search of a Fairy,
Whose Rozez he knowzez
Were not honeyed for he,
But to breathe a sweet incense
To solace the Princess
Of far-away Zzzee.

WALTER DE LA MARE
1873–1956

From Beavers, Bees should learn to mend their ways:
A Bee just Works; a Beaver Works and Plays.

ARTHUR GUITERMAN, *A Poets Proverbs*, 1924

Bee-Master

This is the bee-master's reckoning
In England. Walk among the hives and hear. . . .

Forget not bees in winter, though they sleep,
For winter's big with summer in her womb,
And when you plant your rose-trees, plant them deep,
Having regard to bushes all aflame,
And see the dusky promise of their bloom
In small red shoots, and let each redolent name—
Tuscany, Crested Cabbage, Cottage Maid—
Load with full June November's dank repose;
See the kind cattle drowsing in the shade,
And hear the bee about his amorous trade,
Brown in the gipsy crimson of the rose.

In February, if the days be clear,
The waking bee, still drowsy on the wing,
Will guess the opening of another year
And blunder out to seek another spring.
Crashing through winter sunlight's pallid gold,
His clumsiness sets catkins on the willow
Ashake like lambs' tails in the early fold,
Dusting with pollen all his brown and yellow,
But when the rimy afternoon turns cold
And undern squalls buffet the chilly fellow,
He'll seek the hive's warm waxen welcoming
And set about the chambers' classic mould.

And then pell-mell his harvest follows swift,
Blossom and borage, lime and balm and clover,
On Downs the thyme, on cliffs the scantling thrift,
Everywhere bees go racing with the hours,

63

For every bee becomes a drunken lover,
Standing upon his head to sup the flowers.
All over England, from Northumbrian coasts,
To the wild sea-pink blown on Devon rocks,
Over the merry southern gardens, over
The grey-green bean-fields, round the Kentish oasts
Through the frilled spires of cottage hollyhocks,
Go the big brown fat bees, and wander in
Where dusty spears of sunlight cleave the barn,
And seek the sun again, and storm the whin,
And in the warm meridian solitude
Hum in the heather round the moorland tarn.

Look, too, when summer hatches out the brood,
In tardy May or early June,
And the young queens are strong in the cocoon,
Watch, if the days be warm,
The flitting of the swarm.

Follow, for if beyond your sight they stray,
Your bees are lost, and you must take your way
Homeward disconsolate; but be at hand
And you may take your bees on strangers' land.
Have your skep ready, drowse them with your smoke;
Whether they cluster on the handy bough
Or in the difficult hedge, be nimble now,
For bees are captious folk
And quick to turn against the lubber's touch,
But if you shake them to their wicker hutch
Firmly, and turn towards the hive your skep,
Into the hive the clustered thousands stream,
Mounting the little slatted sloping step,
A ready colony, queen, workers, drones,
Patient to build again the waxen thrones
For younger queens, and all the chambered cells
For lesser brood, and all the immemorial scheme.

And still they labour, though the hand of man
Inscrutable and ravaging descends,
Pillaging in their citadels,
Defeating wantonly their provident plan,
Making a havoc of their patient hoard;
Still silly bees, not knowing to what end,
Not knowing to what ultimate reward
Or what new ruin of the garnered hive
The senseless god in man will send,
Still in blind stupid industry to strive,
Constructing for destruction pitiably,
That still their unintelligible lord
May reap his wealth from their calamity.

V. SACKVILLE-WEST
1892–1962

THE PROFITABLE BEE

Who so keepe well Sheepe and Been,
Sleepe or wake, their thrift comes in.

If bees swarm in May they're worth a pound next day.

When Mrs Gorm (Aunt Eloise)
Was stung to death by savage bees,
Her husband (Prebendary Gorm)
Put on his veil and took the swarm.
He's publishing a book, next May,
On 'How to Make Bee-keeping Pay'.

HARRY GRAHAM
1874–1936

As profitable, laborious, loiall, swift, nimble, quick of feet,
bold, cunning, chaste, neat, browne, chillie, as a bee.

The author's father, James Bonner, was, like himself, fond of
rearing bees, and often had a dozen of hives at a time in his
garden. He lived about fifty years in the married state, and had
twelve children, of whom the author is the youngest alive. He
frequently boasted that, in good seasons, he made as much
money by his bees as nearly to purchase oatmeal sufficient to
serve his numerous family for the whole year. He purchased a
large quarto Bible with the wax produced in one year from his
hives, which served as a family book ever after; and his house
was always well supplied with honey, and a kind of weak mead,
which served for drink at all seasons of the year.

Bonner's *New Plan for Increasing the
Number of Bee-Hives in Scotland*, 1795

A swarm of bees in May
Is worth a load of hay;
A swarm of bees in June
Is worth a silver spoon;
A swarm of bees in July
Is not a worth a fly.

TRADITIONAL

The Bee-keeper

In the plain of the world's dust like a great Sea,
The golden thunders of the Lion and the Honey-Bee
In the Spirit, held with the Sun a Colloquy

Where an old woman stood—thick Earthiness—
Half Sun, half Clod,
A plant alive from the root, still blind with earth
And all the weight of Death and Birth.

She, in her primitive dress
Of clay, bent to her hives
And heard her sisters of the barren lives

Begin to stir . . . the Priestesses of the Gold Comb
Shaped by Darkness, and the Prophetesses
Who from a wingless pupa, spark of gold

In the Dark, rose with gold bodies bright as the Lion,
And the trace of the Hand of God on ephemeral wings
To sing the great Hymn of Being to the Lost:

'This Earth is the honey of all Beings, and all Beings
Are the honey of this Earth . . . O bright immortal Lover
That is incarnate in the body's earth—
O bright immortal Lover Who is All!'

'This Water is the honey of all Beings, and all Beings
Are the honey of this Water . . . O the bright immortal Lover
That is in water and that is the seed
Of Life . . . O bright immortal Lover Who is All!'

'This Fire is the honey of all Beings, and all Beings
Are the honey of this Fire . . . O bright immortal Lover
That is in fire and shines in mortal speech—
O bright immortal Lover Who is All!'

'This Air is the honey of all Beings, and all Beings
Are the honey of this Air . . . O bright immortal Lover
That is in air and is our Being's breath—
O bright immortal Lover Who is All!'

'This Sun is the honey of all Beings, and all Beings
Are the honey of this Sun . . . O bright immortal Lover
That is in the sun and is our Being's sight—
O bright immortal Lover Who is All!'

'This Thunder is the honey of all Beings, and all Beings
Are the honey of this Thunder . . . O the bright immortal Lover,
That is in thunder and all voices—the beasts' roar—
Thunder of rising saps—the voice of Man!
O bright immortal Lover Who is All!'

This was the song that came from the small span
Of thin gold bodies shaped by the holy Dark . . .

And the old woman in her moral dress of clay
(That plant alive from the root, still thick with earth)
Felt all the saps of Day.

And in the plain of dust like a great Sea
The Lion in the Spirit cried, 'Destroy—destroy
The old and wrinkled Darkness.' But the Sun
—That great gold simpleton—laughed like a boy,
And kissed the old woman's cheek and blessed her clay.

The great Sun laughed, and dancing over Chaos,
Shouts to the dust 'O mortal Lover! Think what wonders
May be born of our love—what golden heroes!'

The Bee in the Spirit said: 'The gold combs lay
In the cold rock and the slain Lion, amid spent golden thunders.

EDITH SITWELL
1887–1964

69

Bowes—Beer—Bees

Old beeman Bowes of Buttercup Leas,
His pleasure was beer and his business was bees
In Barleymow Parish was never a swarm
That Bowes did not handle without any harm.

He never wore gloves and he never wore veil
For the bees loved Bowes and the smell of his ale
From roof or from steeple, from bush or from tree
Without any harm he would charm every bee.
They would lie around his neck without stinging or stir
As soft and as warm as a collar of fur.
Oft he was seen staggering home half seas over,
Humming with bees like a paddock of clover.
Creeping and crawling inside his cravat,
As blind as a piper as full as a vat.

There came a new man to the old 'Bread and Cheese'
As did not know Bowes and his booze and his bees
And when the old buffer came into the room
A buzzing with bees like a beanfield in bloom,
The barman he pointed the way to the door,
'You've had enough beer, so you can't have no more.'

But Bowes replied when these words he did hear,
'A'll give thee bees if tha won't give me beer.'
Then he opened his shirt, where the swarm on his breast
Lay snuggling and warm like a bird in a nest.
The Barman he swore and he swiped with a clout,
But t'was he and not Bowes and his bees as went out.

ANON AUSTRALIAN BEE KEEPER

71

The Triolet

The bees are glad the livelong day,
For lilacs in their beauty blow
And make my garden glad and gay.

The bees are glad the livelong day,
They to my blossoms wing their way,
And honey steal from flowers aglow.
The bees are glad the livelong day,
For lilacs in their beauty blow.

DYLAN THOMAS
1914–1953

72

The Beekeeper's Daughter

A garden of mouthings. Purple, scarlet-speckled, black
The great corollas dilate, peeling back their silks.
Their musk encroaches, circle after circle,
A well of scents almost too dense to breathe in.
Hieratical in your frockcoat, maestro of the bees,
You move among the many breasted hives,

My heart under your foot, sister of a stone.

Trumpet-throats open to the beaks of birds.
The Golden Rain tree drips its powders down.
In these little boudoirs streaked with orange and red
The anthers nod their heads, potent as kings
To father dynasties. The air is rich.
Here is a queenship no mother can contest—

A first that's death to taste: dark flesh, dark parings.

In burrows narrow as a finger, solitary bees
Keep house among the grasses. Kneeling down
I set my eye to a hole-mouth and meet an eye
Round, green, disconsolate as a tear.
Father, bridegroom, in this Easter egg
Under the coronal of sugar roses

The queen bee marries the winter of your year.

SYLVIA PLATH
1932–1963

73

Wild Bees

Often in summer on a tarred bridge plank standing
Or downstream between willows, a safe Ophelia drifting
In a rented boat—I had seen them come and go,
Those wild bees swift as tigers, their gauze wings a-glitter
In passionless industry, clustering black at the crevice
Of a rotten cabbage tree, where their hive was hidden low.

But never strolled too near. Till one half-cloudy evening
Of ripe January, my friends and I
Came, gloved and masked to the eyes like plundering
    desperadoes
To smoke them out. Quiet beside the stagnant river
We trod wet grasses down, hearing the crickets chitter
And waiting for light to drain from the wounded sky.

Before we reached the hive their sentries saw us
And sprang invisible through the darkening air;
Stabbed, and died in stinging. The hive woke. Poisonous
    fuming
Of sulphur filled the hollow trunk, and crawling
Blue flame sputtered: yet still their suicidal
Live raiders dived and clung to our hands and hair.

O it was Carthage under the Roman torches
Or loud with flames and falling timber, Troy.
A job well botched: half of the honey melted
And half the rest young grubs. Through earth-black
    smouldering ashes
And maimed bees groaning, we drew out our plunder—
Little enough their gold, and slight our joy.

Fallen then the city of instinctive wisdom.
Tragedy is written distinct and small:
A hive burned on a cool night in summer.

But loss is a precious stone to me, a nectar
Distilled in time, preaching the truth of winter
To the fallen heart that does not cease to fall.

JAMES K. BAXTER
1926–1972

Bees

From the hollow trees in their native home
them old fellows cut the honeycomb.
On honey an' little white grubs they fed,
'cause them young bees was blackfellers' bread.
That's why they was so mighty and strong
in their native home in Currarong.
An them old fellers' drink was honey-bul:
honey an' water, a coolamon[†] full.   *wooden carrying dish
Naked through the bush they went,   used by aborigines*
an' never knew what sickness meant.
Them native bees could do you no harm,
they'd crawl all over your honey-smeared arm.
But them Eyetalian bees, they'd bung
your eyes right up. When we was young
we used to rob their honey-trees.
Savage! They'd fetch your blood. Them bees
would zoom an zing an' chase a feller
from Bombaderry to Bodalla.
Well, old Uncle Minah, old Billy Bulloo,
old Jacky Mumbulla, King Merriman too,
them fierce old fellers, they're all gone now.
An' the wild honey's still in the gumtree bough.

Related by Percy Mumbulla to Roland Robinson

HONEY

Honey is like the morning sun
It has all the grace of summer
And the mellow freshness of the fall

GARCIA LORCA
1899–1936

It's a mighty poor bee that doesn't make more honey than he
wants.

TRADITIONAL, JAMAICA

Honey is the epic of love
The materialization of the infinite
The soul and the blood of flowers
Condensed through the spirit of others.

GARCIA LORCA
1899–1936

SING A SONG OF HONEY

Honey from the white rose, honey from the red,
Is not that a pretty thing to spread upon your bread?
When the flower is open, the bee begins to buzz,
I'm very glad, I'm very glad, I'm very glad it does—
Honey from the lily,
    Honey from the May,
And the daffodilly,
    And the lilac spray—
When the snow is falling, when the fires are red,
Is not that a pretty thing to spread upon your bread?

Honey from the heather, honey from the lime,
Is not that a dainty thing to eat in winter-time?
Honey from the cherry, honey from the ling,
Honey from the celandine that opens in the Spring.
Honey from the clover,
    Honey from the pear—
Summer may be over,
    But I shall never care.
When the fires are blazing, honey from the lime
Makes a very dainty dish to eat in winter-time.

Kings will leave their counting any time they're told
Queens are in the parlour spreading honey gold,
Gold from honeysuckle, gold from lupins' spire—
Who will stay in counting-house and miss the parlour fire?
Honey from the daisy,
    Honey from the plum,
Kings will all be lazy,
    And glad that Winter's come.
Who will keep to counting till the sum is told?
I'll be in the parlour and eating honey-gold.

BARBARA EUPHAN TODD

The Bees

Then to the bees one said,
'Knowledge from us is fled;
The stream is grown impure,
Nought that we say is sure;

Come you, unto our aid,
Come, sages, honey-fed;
You who roam far and wide,
Many-winged, many eyed.
Who, out of all your sort,
Show the most anxious thought,
Building the sixfold cell
Wondrously, very well;
You, who in honeyed dark
Brood on the mystery stark
Of birth and death and pain
And of re-birth again.

For whom were these things done?
For whom still shines the sun?
For whom does dew descend?
For whom the winter end?
Is it not all for men?
Make our minds proud again.
Are we not last of things?
Have we not also wings,
And do we not one day
Spread them and pass away?'

His little friends replied,
'Wisdom with you has died.
Only the bees have souls.
Even in trees and holes
Of wood the wild bees know

78

More than your words now show.
Is not the world a field
Spread in the sun to yield
Honey and scent and dew,
Its share of labour too?
Is not night sent to cool
The too-warm liquid pool
Of golden sweetness, day
Only to show the way
To lonely flowers which
Hide in a far-off ditch?
And is not heaven indeed
Rather another mead,
Untouched by time, unseen,
A hedge for ever green,
Seasonless, always spring
And early summer, a thing
Hid in the future, yet
Surer than autumns wet?
This is our hope, and we
Hold it in certainty
Though the hive leak and though
Winter and rain and snow
Break through the vaulting high
And send us out to die
Wingless upon the hill,
That field awaits us still,
And from the yellow sod
The bees return to God.'

MONK GIBBON
b. 1896

79

BEESWAX

The calf, the goose, the bee,
  The world is ruled by these three
Meaning that waxe, pennes, and parchments sway all men's
    states.

JOH. GWILLIM, 1565–1621

Hollow Tooth, to stop:

Warm by the fire a little bees'-wax, and with the finger and
thumb work it into a soft paste: fill the tooth with it, and it will
often give relief from pain, and stay in quite as long as many of
the pastes which are advertised for stopping teeth, and may very
easily be renewed.

HOUSEHOLD RECIPES

As wax increases in the hive, so give us all good fortune.

To prevent snow water or rain from penetrating the soles of shoes or boots in winter:

This simple and effectual remedy is nothing more than a little beeswax and mutton suet, warmed in a pipkin, until in a liquid state; then rub some of it slightly over the edges of the sole where the stitches are, which will repel the wet, and not in the least prevent the blacking from having its usual effect.

THE FAMILY RECEIPT BOOK, Pittsburgh, 1819

Honey and wax furnish mankind with the two noblest of things
    which are sweetness and light.

JONATHAN SWIFT
1667–1745

The Bees

Bees over the gooseberry bushes,
Bees with golden thighs
Climbing out of pale flowers
(Bees singing to you for a long while,
You sitting quite still,
Holding the sun in your lap),
Bees, take care!
You may catch fire in the sun,
If you venture so high in the blue air.

LOLA RIDGE
1883–1941

The Arrival of the Bee Box

I ordered this, this clean wood box
Square as a chair and almost too heavy to lift.
I would say it was the coffin of a midget
Or a square baby
Were there not such a din in it.

The box is locked, it is dangerous.
I have to live with it overnight
And I can't keep away from it.
There are no windows, so I can't see what is in there.
There is only a little grid, no exit.

I put my eye to the grid.
It is dark, dark,
With the swarmy feeling of African hands
Minute and shrunk for export,
Black on black, angrily clambering.

82

How can I let them out?
It is the noise that appals me most of all,
The unintelligible syllables.
It is like a Roman mob,
Small, taken one by one, but my god, together!

I lay my ear to furious Latin.
I am not a Caesar.
I have simply ordered a box of maniacs.
They can be sent back.
They can die, I need feed them nothing, I am the owner.

I wonder how hungry they are.
I wonder if they would forget me
If I just undid the locks and stood back and turned into a tree.
There is the laburnum, its blond colonnades,
And the petticoats of the cherry.

They might ignore me immediately
In my moon suit and funeral veil.
I am no source of honey
So why should they turn on me?
Tomorrow I will be sweet God, I will set them free.

The box is only temporary.

SYLVIA PLATH
1932–1963

BEARS AND BEES

Where there is honey the bears come uninvited.

The Bear and the Bees

The woodland creatures held election
To fill the office for inspection
Of honey-hives; in early spring
The candidates came mustering;
All others were rejected,
Mishka put in his nose and—was elected.
You'll say the choice was somewhat funny,
Since Mishka was a whale for honey.

Think as you will,
    Wild creatures are wild creatures still.
Mishka the honey pinched, and in his cave
He hid it safe, the hoary knave.
And then began a-fussing and a-fuming,
Accusing and condemning and subsuming,
And Mishka got the sack,
But no one got their honey back.
The court confirmed their own decision,
    But, in derision,
Mishka, old ruffian, never flicked an ear,
    With conscience clear,
He for a season to his cave withdraws.
There, soft and warm, he sucks his honeyed paws,
To the world and its temptations bids adieu,
'To-morrow to fresh woods and pastures new.'

The Book of the Bear, Nonesuch Press, 1926
A Krylov fable translated from the Russian
by Jane Harrison and Hope Mirrlees

He who shareth honey with the bear hath the least part of it.

GERMAN

Winnie-the-Pooh sang a little song to himself. It went like this:

> Isn't it funny
> How a bear likes honey?
> Buzz! Buzz! Buzz!
> I wonder why he does.

Then he climbed a little farther . . . and a little farther . . . and then just a little farther. By that time he had thought of another song.

> It's a very funny thought that, if Bears were Bees,
> They'd build their nests at the *bottom* of trees.
> And that being so (if the Bees were Bears),
> We shouldn't have to climb up all these stairs.

A. A. MILNE
1882–1956

According to the theory of aerodynamics, and as may be readily demonstrated by means of a wind tunnel, the bumble-bee is unable to fly. This is because the size, weight, and shape of his body in relation to the total wing span make flight impossible. But the bumble-bee, being ignorant of these scientific facts and possessing considerable determination, does fly—and makes a little honey, too.

FRANCIS CLIFFORD, *The Naked Runner*, 1966

86

The Bee

A zig-zag bee, zzz and zzz-ing, came
Out of the flowers in my room; his claim
For being there was he had been carried there
While he worked in a flower, unaware.

He swayed, buzzed toward a window where a screen
Stopped him, sieved the universe between
A green beyond and his desire for
A green beyond: he was neither/nor.

From flowers to screen, he hummed a sort of thunder—
Nothing, yet olympic to my wonder;
His song stopped when the network stopped the bee.
He inspected man's ingenuity.

The screen was there to keep him out, not in.
I wanted to let his ecstasy begin
Again—to let it continue as it was.
Let a bee have his summer: what he does

With his brief season is a song for hours;
Let a bee have his privilege of flowers,
I thought. Therefore, I took an envelope
(He did not know this was his one white hope)

And tried to manoeuver him to crawl inside.
Something, maybe fear or maybe pride,
Prompted him to be difficult:
He had his bee-wise reason to consult

Whether this should be or should not be.
I learned some independence from the bee.
Yet, because I could not watch him strive
Futilely, and wanted him alive—

I could not let him die, with honeysuckle
Just in view—I nudged him with my knuckle,
Then carried him outside like a note for mailing;
I opened the envelope, and the bee went sailing

Into his freedom as his thunder began
Again. I felt aliveness as a man
Should. I felt the summer rise in me.
I saw a million flowers for the bee.

JOHN FANDEL
1925–

The Bee

The bee is a merchant.
He trades among
flower planets.

PETER KELSO, aged 12

Potted
Wintering

Queen right,
Workers infinite,
Winter store,
Galore,
Quiet spot,
No knock,
Roof dry,
Go bee-bye.

The Beemaster's Prayer

Will there be Bees in heavenly places
        Will there be Bees?

Winging their way through the golden spaces
To fruitify the eternal trees
That yield their sweet life-giving store
Month by month for evermore.

Will soft Bee music haunt the stream
Whose waters shine with crystal glow
And will they come where lilies gleam
To sip the eternal nectar flow?

Lord thou didst love our earthly places
Birds and flowers and shady trees—
Let there be Bees in heavenly places
        Let there be Bees.

ANON

Erected by voluntary contribution by the inhabitants of Dundonald Village and Neighbourhood, in memory of John Templeton, who died 27 August, 1899, aged 72.

Dundonald folk noo miss him sair,
Frae his kind acts they'll hae nae mair,
He lived a long, unselfish life,
And noo lies here freed from all strife.
The busy bees 'll miss him, tae,
When they cast off what will they due?
He'll no be there when they flee oot,
To drum them back 'neath his white cloot.

GOD SAVE THE QUEEN!

INDEX

of authors and first lines

A Bee his burnished Carriage	59
A bee upon a briar-rose hung	54
A busy humble bee am I	22
A garden of mouthings. Purple, scarlet-speckled, black	73
A golden bee a-cometh	54
A Knight of a gay and a gallant mien	58
A play o' bees in May's worth a noble the same day	56
A swarm of bees in May	57, 67
A zig-zag bee, zzz and zzz-ing came	87
Ah, see where, robb'd and murder'd in that pit	24
All hands employ'd, the royal work grows warm	19
And from the knotted flowers of thyme	49
Antiphilus of Byzantium	11
As Julia once a-slumb'ring lay	20
Baxter, James K. (New Zealand poet, critic, playwright)	74
Bees! Bees! Hark to your bees!	40
Bees, of Bees of Paradise	55
Bees over the gooseberry bushes	82
Behold those winged images!	47
Blount, Thomas	23
Bunyan, John	19
Charm'd with a drink which Highlanders compose	60
Chaucer, Geoffrey	13
Child of patient industry	30
Churchill, Charles	52
Clare, John	49
Claridge, John	32
Clifford, Frances	86
Combe, William	45
Cupid once upon a bed	46
Day Lewis, C.	14
de la Mare, Walter	62
Dickinson, Emily (US poet)	i, 59
Dryden, John	19
Dundonald folk noo miss him sair	90
Fandel, John (US poet)	87
Fergusson, Robert (Scots poet)	25
Freneau, Philip ('Poet of the American Revolution')	28

From Beavers, Bees should learn to mend their ways 62
From the hollow trees in their native home 75

Gibbon, Monk (Irish writer and critic) 78
God's little epigrams, the Bees 37
Graham, Harry 66
Grahame 56
Gray, Thomas 60
Great God Almighty in thy pretty Bee 18
Guiterman, Arthur 62
Gwillim, Joh. 80

Harrison, Jane 84
Herds, blythsome tune your canty reeds 25
Here is the place; right over the hill 38
Herrick, Robert 20, 51
Honey bees, honey bees, hear what I say 42
Honey from the white rose, honey from the red 77
Honey is like the morning sun 76
Honey is the epic of love 76
Hood, Thomas 60
How does the little busy bee 16
Hurdis, James 29, 45

I eat my peas with honey 45
I ordered this, this clean wood box 82
If rain threatens, be sure they'll not roam too far afield 33
If thou hast found an honie-combe 51
In the name of the bee i
In the plain of the world's dust like a great Sea 68

Kelso, Peter 88
Kipling, Rudyard 40
Kirk, Richard 37

Lawson, William 57
Lear, Edward 37
Lincoln, Abraham 51
Lorca, Garcia 76
Lovely, aerial blessing, which the bees 11
Lyly, John 13

Madam, the ancient proverb says 45
Magih, Ibn 12
Mantling in the goblet, see 60
Milne, A. A. 86
Milton, John 50
Mirrlees, Hope 84

Moore, Thomas   46
Moorman, F. W.   42

Often in summer on a tarred bridge plank standing   74
Old beeman Bowes of Buttercup Leas   70

Patmore, Coventry   54
Plath, Sylvia (US poet)   73, 82
Pliny the Elder   10
Poring on Caesar's death with earnest eye   53

Queen right   89

Ray, John   21
Ridge, Lola   82
Robinson, Roland (Australian)   75
Rossetti, Christina   17

Sackville-West, V.   51, 63
Shakespeare, William   18
Sitwell, Edith   68
Skipsey, Joseph   54
Smith, Charlotte   30
Smythe, Professor   53
So on a Sabbath morn   56
So work the honey bees   18
Southey, Robert   30
Stevenson, Robert Louis   61
Swift, Jonathan   81

Tennyson, Alfred   51
The bee goes out, and honey home doth bring   19
The bee observe   45
The bees are glad the livelong day   72
The hive is up in arms, expert to teach   52
The pedigree of Honey   59
The woodland creatures held election   84
Then to the bees one said   78
There is a bird of great renown   17
There was an Old Man in a tree   37
This is the bee-master's reckoning   63
Thomas, Dylan   72
Thomson, James   24
Thou art a miser, thou busy busy bee   30
Thou, born to sip the lake or spring   27
Thou cheerful bee! come, freely come   53
Thousandz of thornz there be   62
Todd, Barbara Euphan (US poet)   77

Turner, Charles Tennyson   53

Virgil   14, 33

Watts, Isaac   16
Well then, let me speak of the natural gifts that God himself   14
What does the Bee do?   17
When Mrs Gorm (Aunt Eloise)   66
Where the cherry spreads its flowery tufts   29
Whist! Laatle bees, sad tidings I bear   42
White, Gilbert   44
White virgin honey comes from earliest flowers   51
Whittier, John Greenleaf (US poet)   38
Will there be Bees in heavenly places   89
Willie an' I cam down by Blair   61
Wither, George   18

Amoret Scott's present book stems from her many years as a bee enthusiast and her lifelong interest in collecting books or items connected with country lore or social history. She is a founder member of the Ephemera Society.

Her charming Hampshire garden is filled with old-fashioned plants to encourage bees, butterflies and indolence. As an excellent self-taught cook, honey is a favourite ingredient.

By the same author
Hedgerow Harvest
A selection of old and new recipes, and the lore and wisdom of countryfolk concerning foods found growing in the wild.